DINOSAU
ON THE
MOVE

ARTICULATED PAPER DOLLS TO CUT, COLOR, AND ASSEMBLE

CATHY DIEZ-LUCKIE

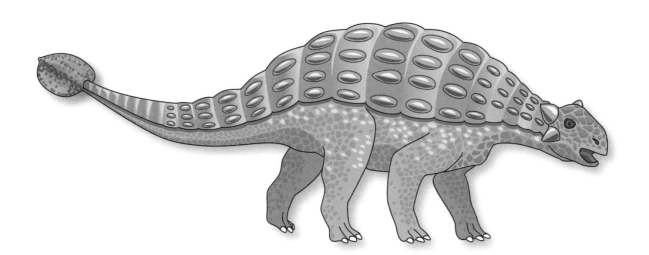

FIGURES IN MOTION

© 2022 Figures In Motion
ISBN 978-1-944481-10-0

1 2 3 4 5 6 7 8 9 10 MERCURY 30 29 28 27 26 25 24 23 22
FIMD-0822

How to Use This Book

For Children...

Make articulated paper dolls of nine dinosaurs and one flying reptile. Cut them out, put them together, and then use your imagination to make them come to life. The figures come in pairs—one waiting for your artistic touches of color and the other ready to cut and assemble.

Make puppets with string, craft sticks, or pipe cleaners, or try producing a stop-motion animation clip using magnets or felt.

For Parents and Educators...

Dinosaurs on the Move provides hands-on activities that will inspire the imagination and creativity of your children, whether they are eager learners who continually want more or reluctant students who need some motivation to learn.

Sharpen your children's storytelling abilities and fine motor skills with dinosaur puppets that come ready to cut and assemble. The figures are printed on sturdy paper and, when assembled with mini brads, are able to really move! Hole punches and mini brads are available at most craft stores and school supply stores as well as at welltrainedmind.com.

Supply your kinesthetic learners with meaningful and easy-to-use activities. Dinosaur days will come alive as children create the moving figures and use them to act out stories. They will also learn fascinating facts about these great creatures: length, weight, habitat, diet, the location of fossil discoveries, and key features are provided for each dinosaur. Use this book independently or combine it with any natural history study.

For Museums and Historical Reenactors...

Inform and educate children about dinosaurs and reptiles as they visit your museum's collection or special exhibition. Let children take home a remembrance of their experience at your museum with *Dinosaurs on the Move*.

This book is dedicated to my father, Blase J. Furfaro. Thank you for your optimism and encouragement in the face of life's difficulties.

With gratitude to Dr. Kenneth Carpenter, former Director and Curator of Paleontology at the Prehistoric Museum USU, for his help in reviewing and editing the information presented in this book.

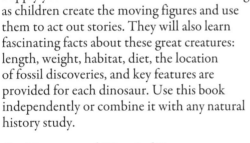

CONTENTS

DINOSAURIA

ALLOSAURUS

Length: 25 to 30 feet (7.5 to 9 meters)

Weight: 4,000 to 6,000 pounds (1,800 to 2,700 kilograms)

Habitat: North American plains

Diet: Carnivore (meat eater)

Fossil Discoveries: Utah, Colorado, Wyoming, Montana, South Dakota, Oklahoma, New Mexico

Features: *Allosaurus* had a massive head with bony ridges over the eyes. Its teeth were serrated and from two to four inches long. It walked on two legs and had short but very strong arms. Each of its hands had three fingers with claws up to six inches long.

ANKYLOSAURUS

Length: 25 to 35 feet (7.5 to 10.5 meters)

Weight: 6,000 to 8,000 pounds (2,700 to 3,600 kilograms)

Habitat: North American woodlands

Diet: Herbivore (plant eater)

Fossil Discoveries: Montana; Wyoming; Alberta, Canada

Features: *Ankylosaurus* was protected in armor consisting of bone plates covered with skin or keratin, a tough protein. The tail had a heavy club at the end made from plates fused to the last few tail vertebrae. *Ankylosaurus* may have used its tail to protect itself from enemies. It had a pair of horns behind each of its eyes. Its skull was large, but it had a very small brain.

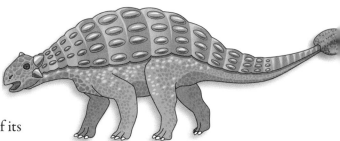

BARYONYX

Length: 25 to 30 feet (7.5 to 9 meters)

Weight: 4,000 pounds (1,800 kilograms)

Habitat: Western European riverbanks

Diet: Piscivore (fish eater)

Fossil Discoveries: England

Features: *Baryonyx* is apparently one of the few dinosaurs that ate fish. It had very large, hook-like claws on the front legs that may have been used to strike at fish in the rivers. The claw on the "thumb" of each hand was about 12 inches long. It had a long, narrow jaw like a crocodile with a total of 96 serrated teeth.

DINOSAURIA

BRACHIOSAURUS

Length: 80 to 100 feet (24 to 30 meters)

Weight: 64,000 to 74,000 pounds (29,000 to 34,000 kilograms)

Habitat: North American woodlands and fern prairies

Diet: Herbivore (plant eater)

Fossil Discoveries: Utah, Colorado

Features: *Brachiosaurus* had a bulky body, a long neck and tail, and a small head with a tiny brain. Its front legs were longer than its hind legs. The nostril opening in the skull was very large and gave the skull a crested look. *Brachiosaurus* was once thought to be the heaviest of all dinosaurs, but paleontologists have found fossils of even heavier dinosaurs such as *Argentinosaurus*.

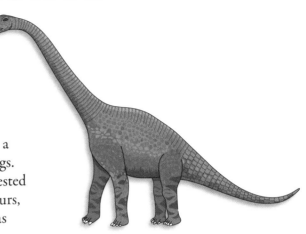

OURANOSAURUS

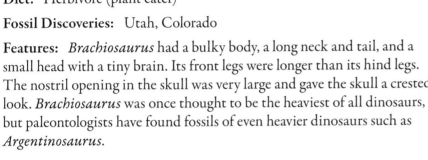

Length: 23 feet (7 meters)

Weight: 8,000 pounds (3,600 kilograms)

Habitat: African floodplain forests of ferns and conifers

Diet: Herbivore (plant eater)

Fossil Discoveries: Niger

Features: *Ouranosaurus* was an iguanodontid dinosaur. It had teeth on the sides of its jaws for chewing tough plant food but not on the front of its snout. Its most notable feature was tall spines that ran along the length of its back and front part of its tail. The spines and associated tendons supported a large skin-covered fin along its back.

PARASAUROLOPHUS

Length: 30 feet (9 meters)

Weight: 5,000 pounds (2,300 kilograms)

Habitat: Western North American rivers and floodplains

Diet: Herbivore (plant eater)

Fossil Discoveries: New Mexico; Utah; Alberta, Canada

Features: *Parasaurolophus* was a hadrosaurid, and was known for its head adornment and ability to walk on two or four legs. It used its beak to bite off plants and chewed the plants with its teeth on the side of its jaw. Some scientists think that its hollow head crest containing a labyrinth of air cavities may have been an instrument for creating sound or for visual recognition of members of its own species.

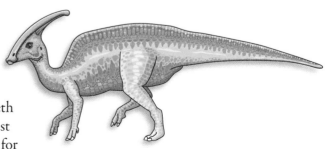

DINOSAURIA

PTERANODON

Wingspan: Up to 26 feet (8 meters)

Weight: 55 pounds (25 kg)

Habitat: North American seas

Diet: Piscivore (fish eater)

Fossil Discoveries: Kansas, Wyoming, South Dakota

Features: *Pteranodon* was a flying reptile (not a dinosaur) that was closely related to the dinosaurs. It ate mostly fish with its toothless beak. Its light wings were covered with a leathery membrane that stretched between its legs, body, and fourth finger. Some *Pteranodon* had a notable head crest.

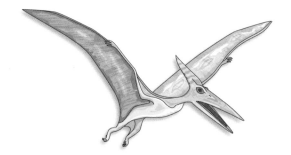

STEGOSAURUS

Length: 20 to 30 feet (6 to 9 meters)

Weight: 8,000 to 10,000 pounds (3,600 to 4,500 kg)

Habitat: North American woodlands

Diet: Herbivore (plant eater)

Fossil Discoveries: Colorado, Wyoming, Utah, Montana, South Dakota, Oklahoma

Features: *Stegosaurus* was slow moving and probably not aggressive. It had two rows of plates extending along the length of its back that were used for display or heat control. Its head was very small in proportion to its body. Its tail had pairs of spikes approximately two feet long that could have been used for defense or display.

TRICERATOPS

Length: 25 to 30 feet (8 to 9 meters)

Weight: 10,000 to 14,000 pounds (4,500 to 6,400 kg)

Habitat: Western North America

Diet: Herbivore (plant eater)

Fossil Discoveries: Colorado; Wyoming; Montana; South Dakota; Saskatchewan, Canada; Alberta, Canada

Features: *Triceratops* is called a horned-face dinosaur because of its nose and eyebrow horns, which are believed to have been used for displaying dominance, for courtship, or for defense. A bony frill that extended from the rear of its skull gave it a massive head. *Triceratops* had wide feet to spread its weight over a large area.

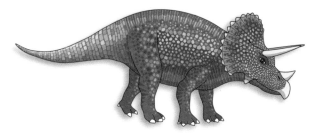

TYRANNOSAURUS REX

Length: 40 feet (12.4 meters)

Weight: 10,000 to 14,000 pounds (4,500 to 6,400 kg)

Habitat: North American woodlands

Diet: Carnivore (meat eater)

Fossil Discoveries: Colorado; Wyoming; Montana; North Dakota; South Dakota; Utah; Saskatchewan, Canada; Alberta, Canada

Features: *Tyrannosaurus rex* was one of the largest carnivores ever to walk the earth. Its skull could be as long as five feet, with closely packed teeth in its upper and lower jaw. Its body was almost parallel to the ground, and its tail extended behind the body to balance its massive head. Its arms were about two feet long with two fingers on each hand.

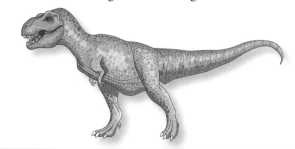

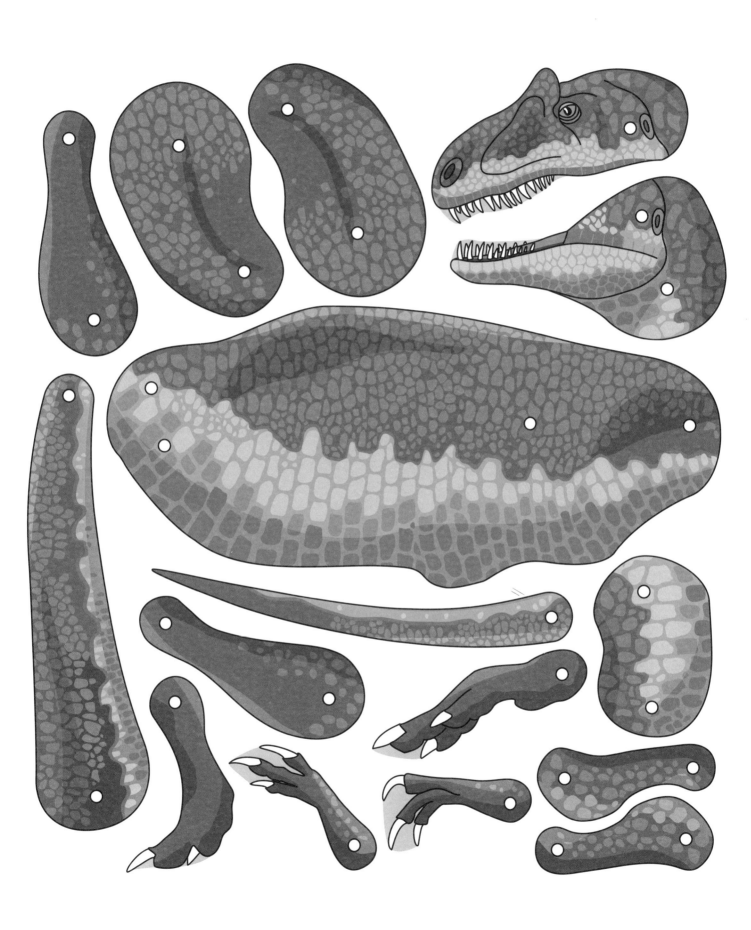

A
Front

H
Front

G
Back

K
Back

A
Back

G
Front

J
Front

J
Back

B
Front

Allosaurus

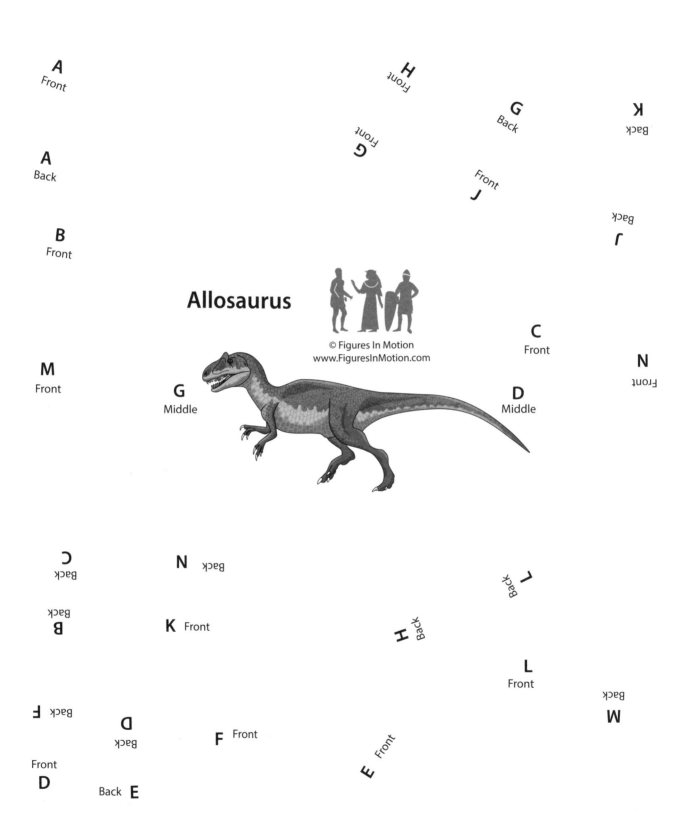

© Figures In Motion
www.FiguresInMotion.com

C
Front

N
Front

M
Front

G
Middle

D
Middle

C
Back

N
Back

J
Back

B
Back

K Front

H Back

L
Front

M
Back

F
Back

D
Back

F Front

E Front

D
Front

E
Back

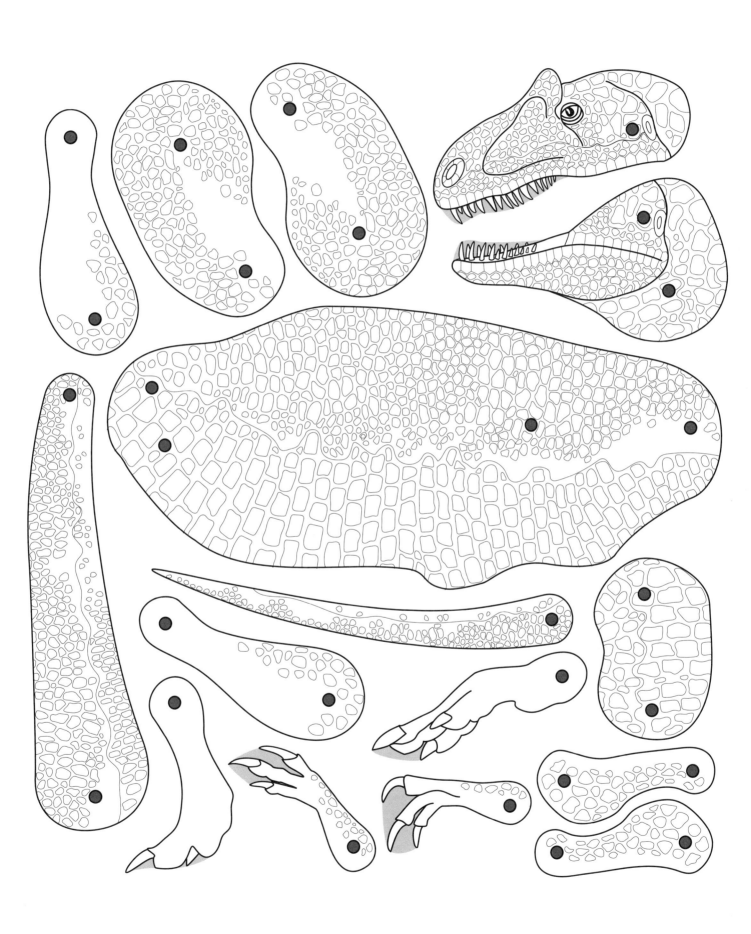

A
Front

A
Back

B
Front

M
Front

Allosaurus

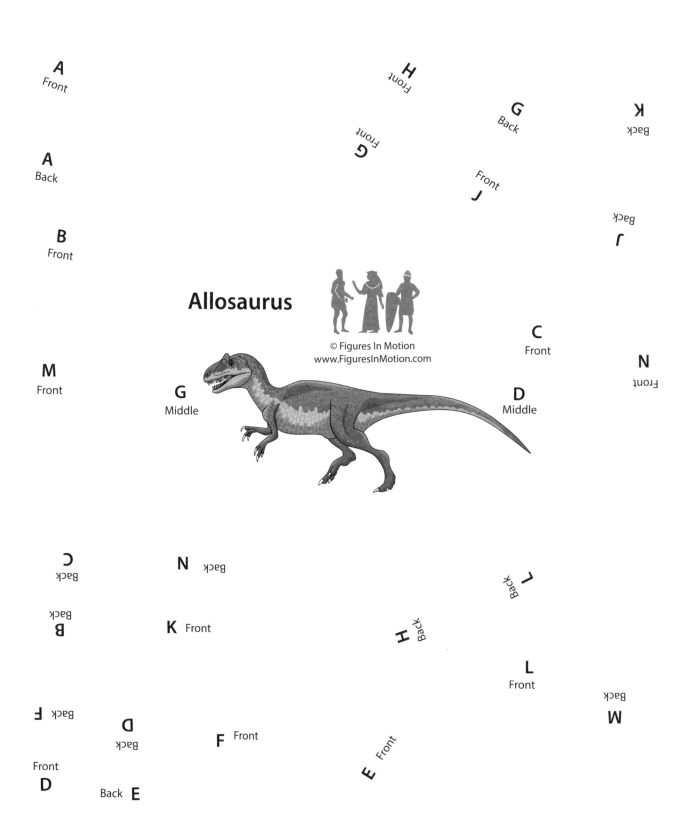

© Figures In Motion
www.FiguresInMotion.com

G
Middle

H
Front

G
Front

G
Back

J
Front

J
Back

K
Back

C
Front

D
Middle

N
Front

C
Back

N
Back

B
Back

K Front

H Back

J
Back

L
Front

D
Front

F
Back

D
Back

F Front

E Front

L
Back

M

Front

D

Back E

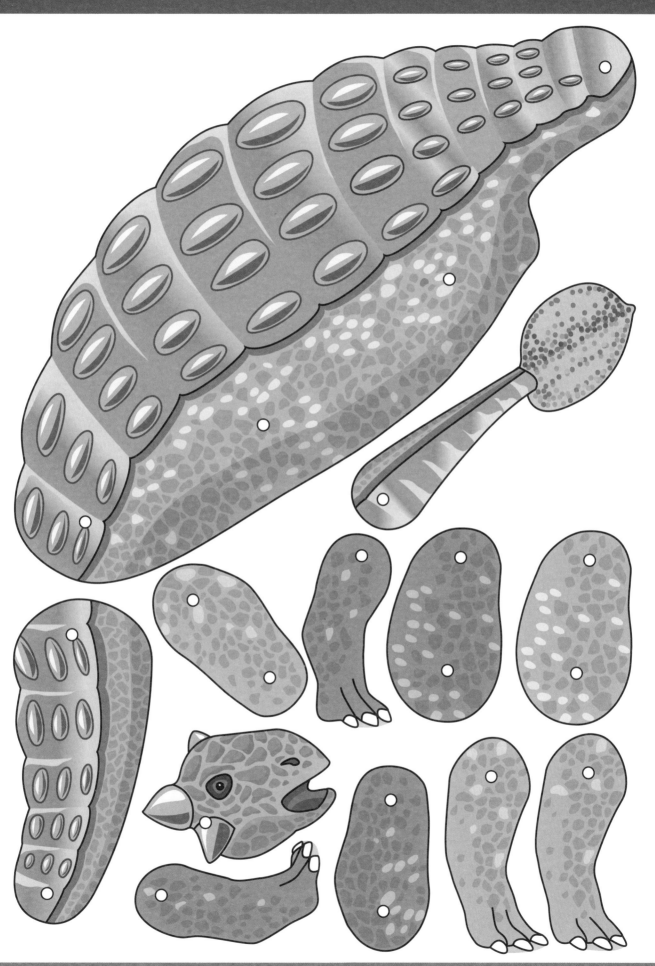

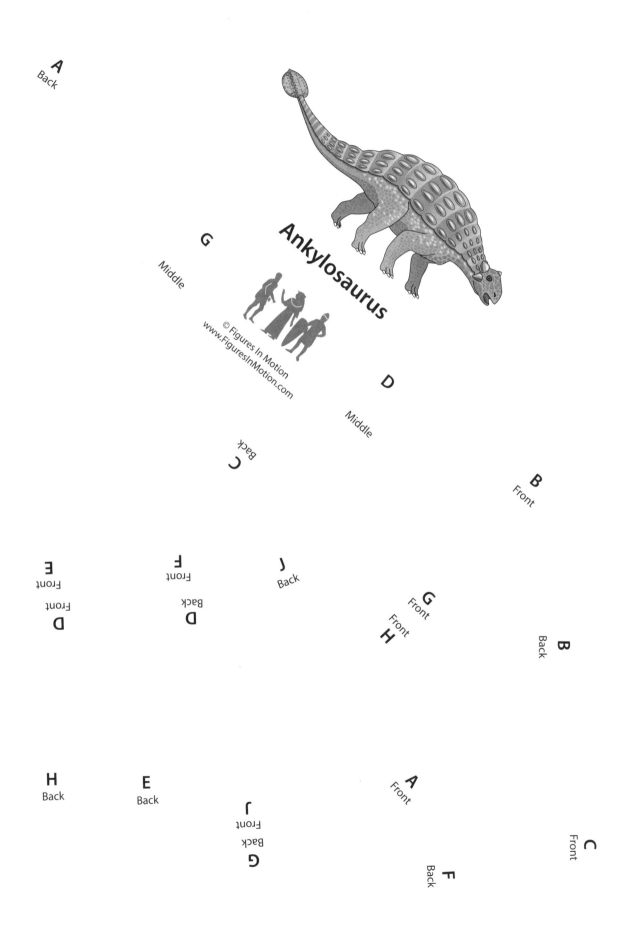

Ankylosaurus

© Figures In Motion
www.FiguresInMotion.com

A
Back

G
Middle

D
Middle

C
Back

B
Front

E
Front

D
Front

F
Front

D
Back

J
Back

G
Front

H
Front

B
Back

H
Back

E
Back

J
Front

G
Back

A
Front

F
Back

C
Front

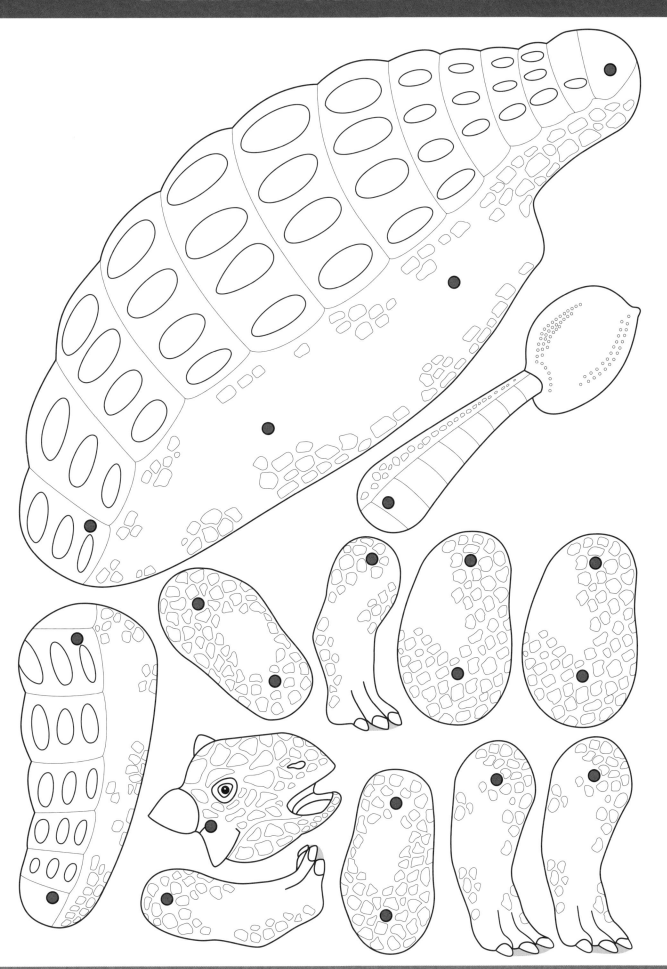

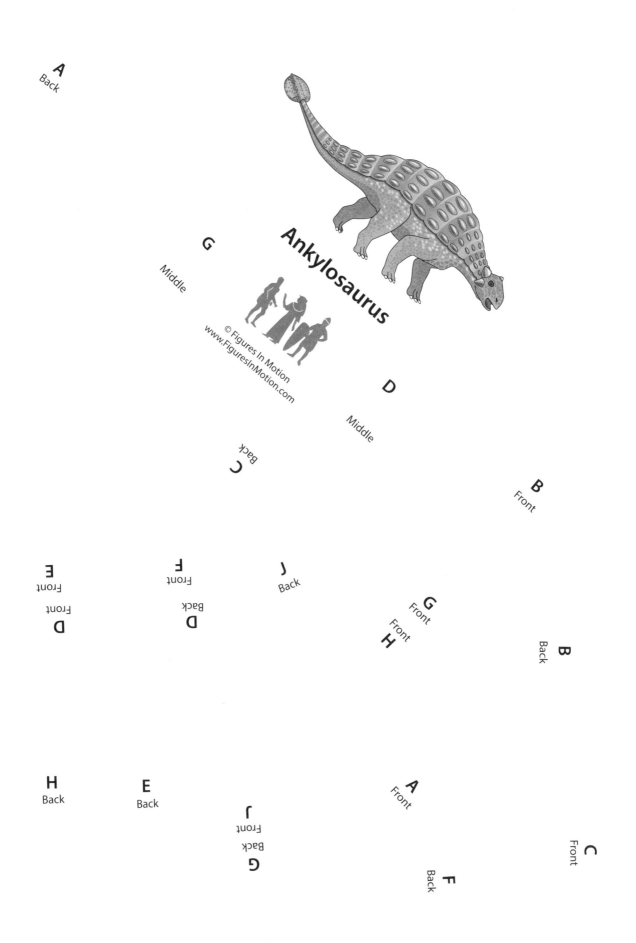

Ankylosaurus

© Figures In Motion
www.FiguresInMotion.com

A
Back

G
Middle

D
Middle

C
Back

B
Front

E
Front

D
Front

F
Front

D
Back

J
Back

G
Front

H
Front

B
Back

H
Back

E
Back

J
Front

G
Back

A
Front

F
Back

C
Front

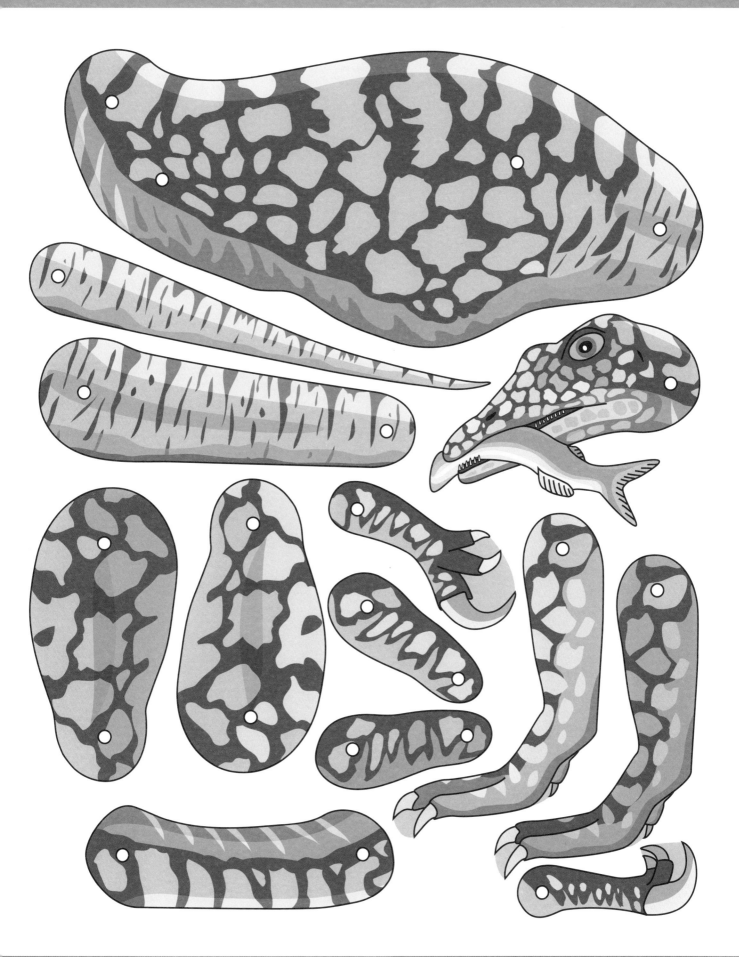

Baryonyx

B
Front

F
Middle

C
Middle

G
Front

K
Back

A
Front

G
Back

K
Front

E
Front

J
Back

J
Front

H
Back

C
Back

F
Back

D
Back

F
Front

H
Front

E
Back

C
Front

A
Back

B
Back

D
Front

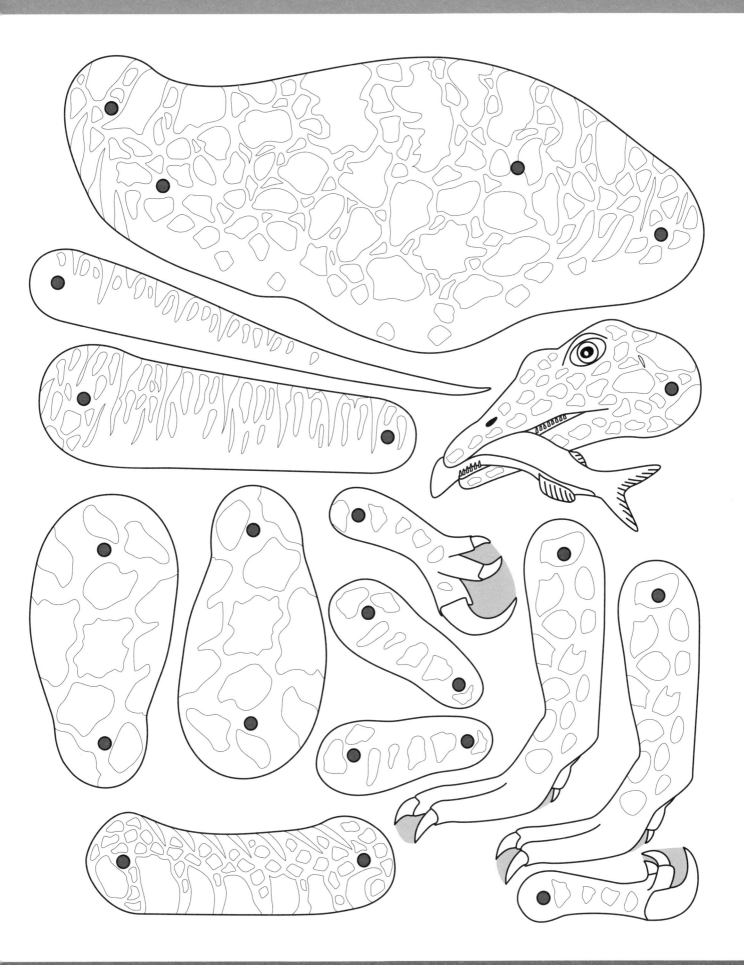

Baryonyx

© Figures In Motion
www.FiguresInMotion.com

F
Middle

B
Front

G
Front

C
Middle

K
Back

A
Front

G
Back

K
Front

E
Front

J
Back

J
Front

F
Back

H
Back

C
Back

D
Back

F
Front

Front
H

E
Back

C
Front

A
Back

B
Back

D
Front

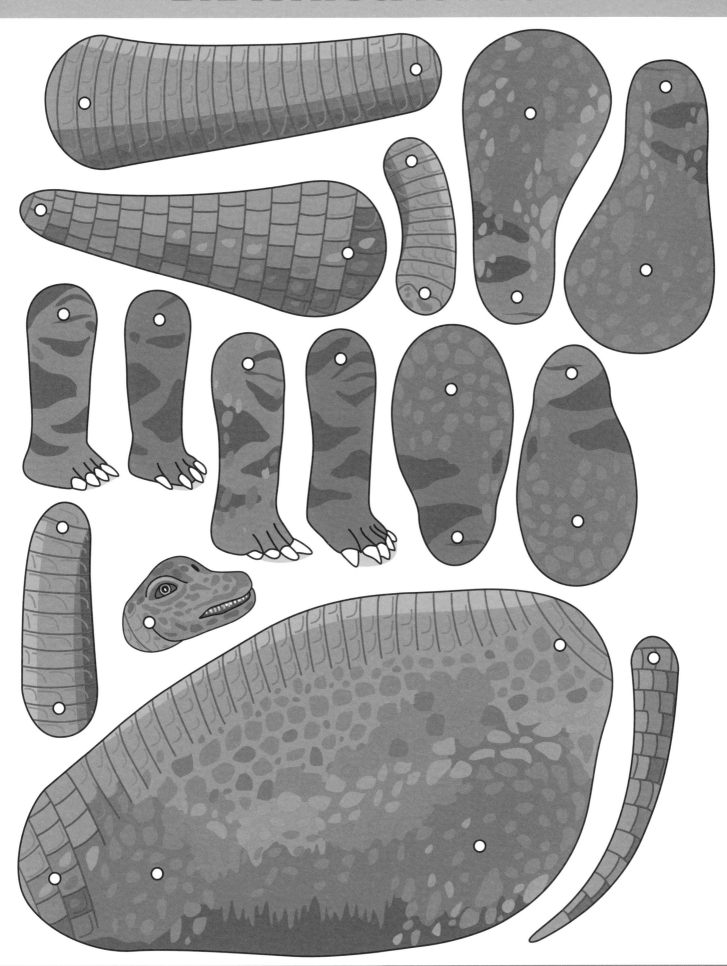

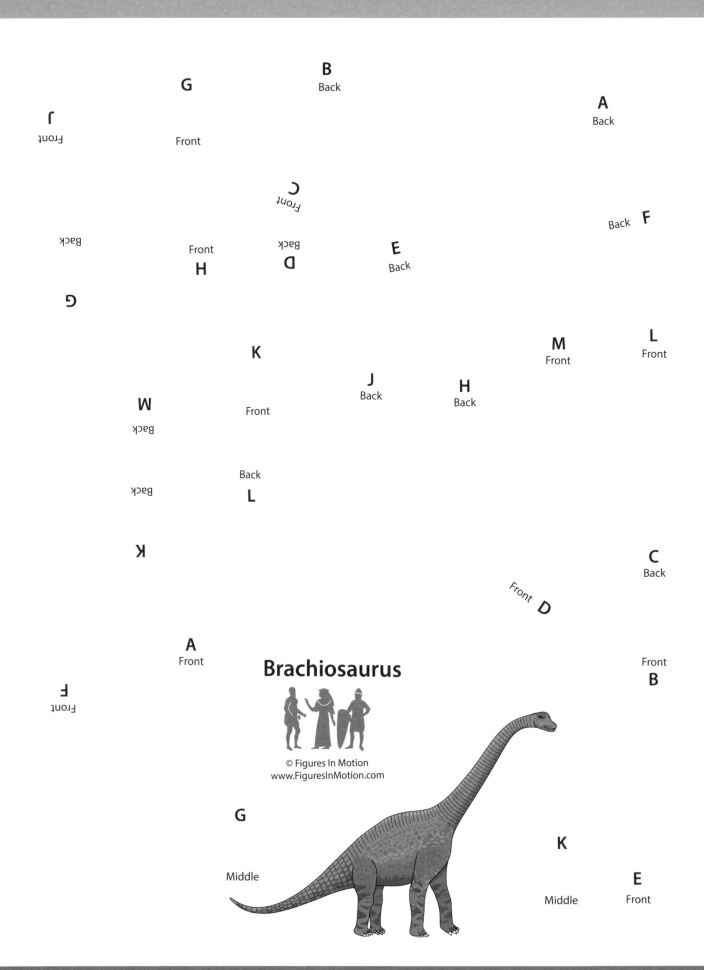

Brachiosaurus

© Figures In Motion
www.FiguresInMotion.com

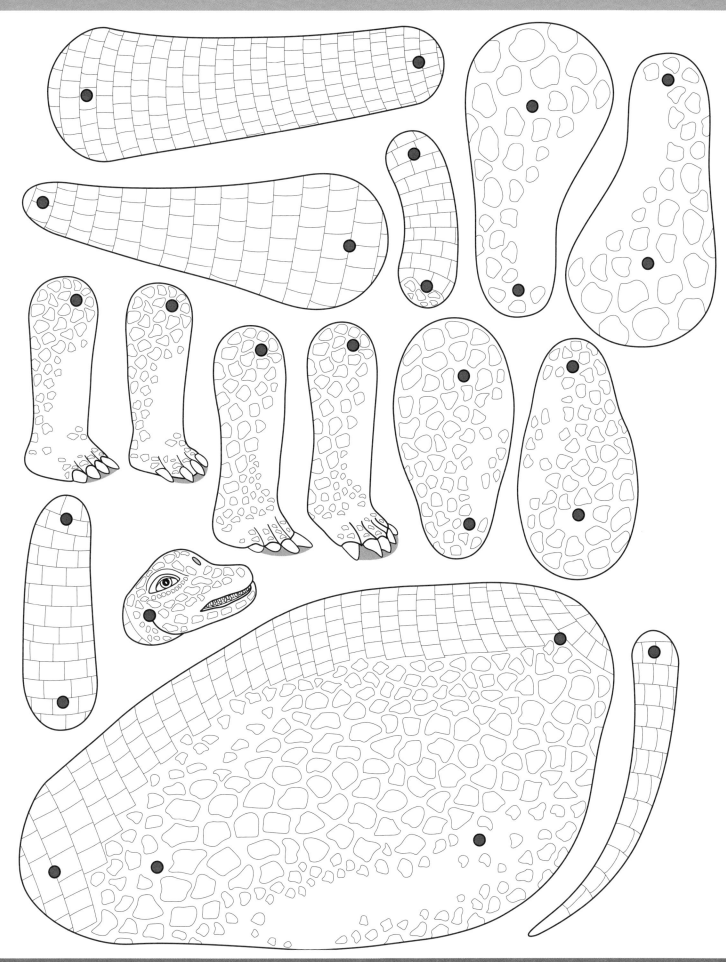

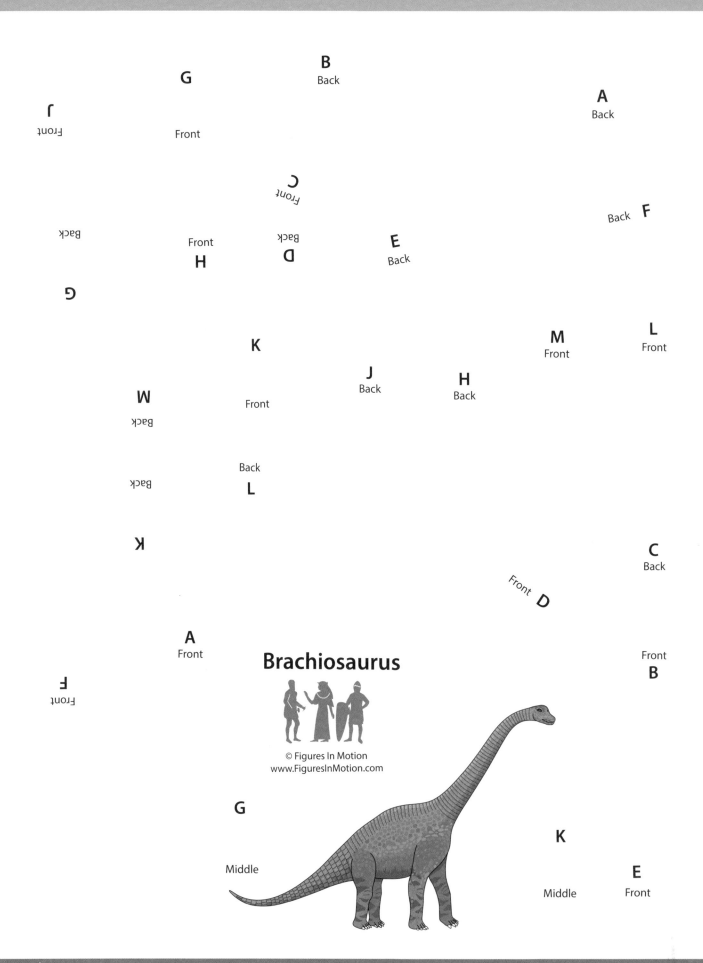

Brachiosaurus

© Figures In Motion
www.FiguresInMotion.com

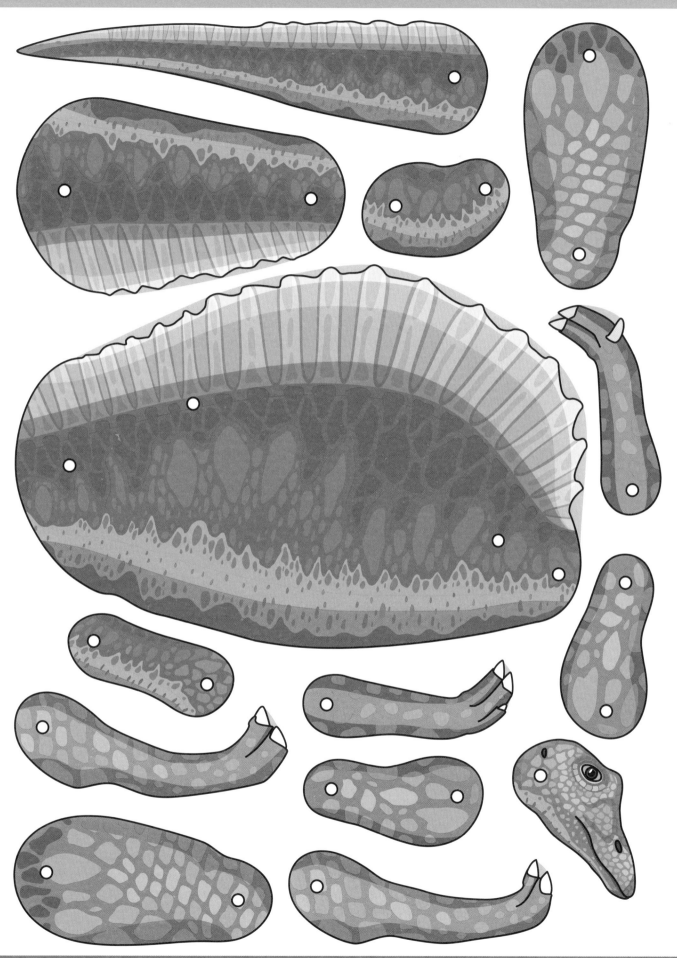

C
Front

E
Back

G
Front

F
Front

A
Back

E
Front

Back
D

B
Front

L
Front

K
Front

B
Front

A
Middle
Front

B
Back

K
Back

L
Back

M
Front

H
Back

H
Front

Back
M

Ouranosaurus

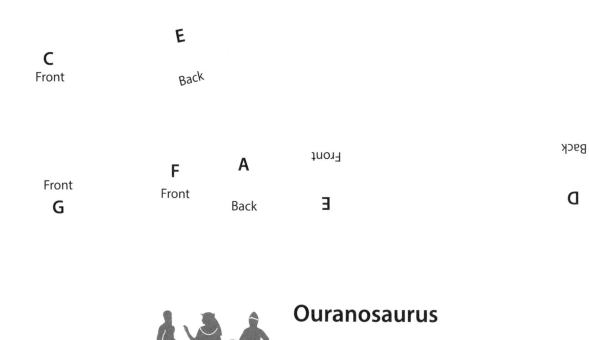
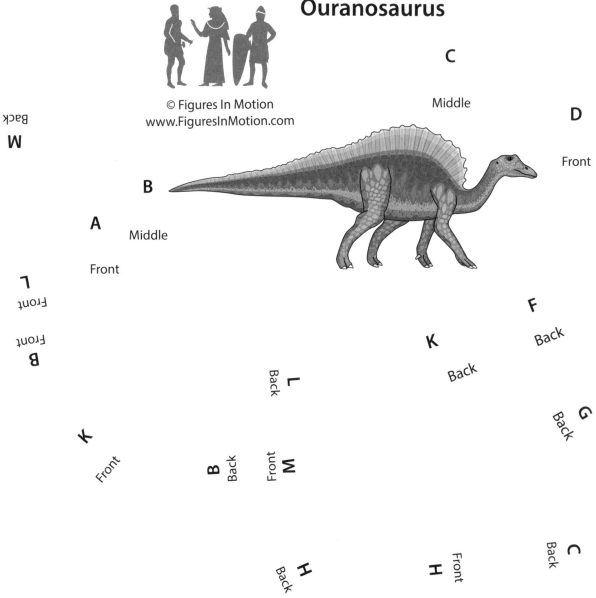

© Figures In Motion
www.FiguresInMotion.com

C
Middle

D
Front

F
Back

G
Back

C
Back

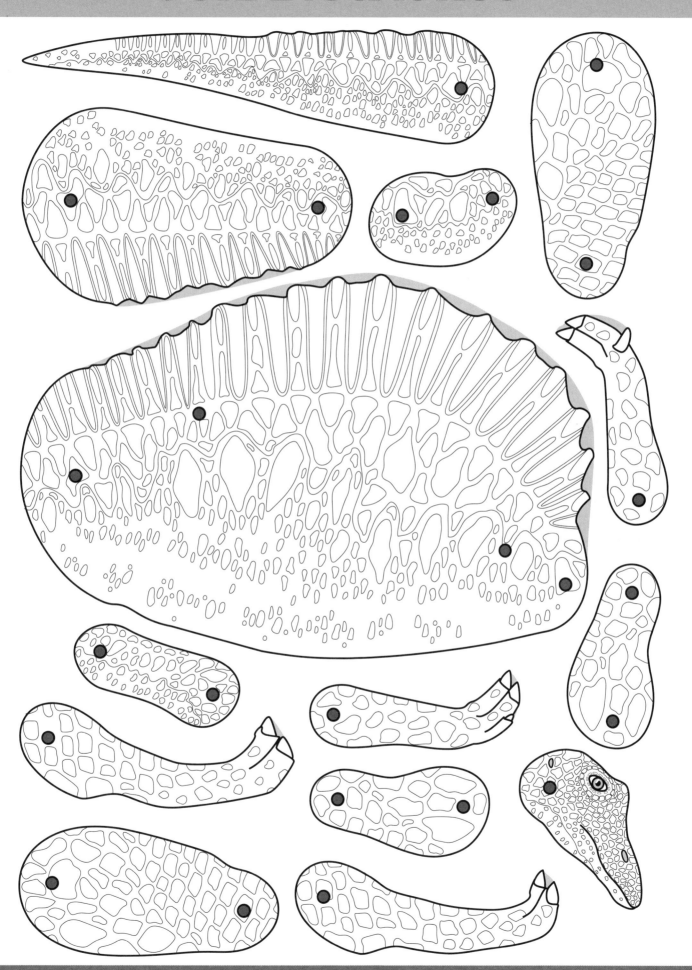

C
Front

E
Back

G
Front

F
Front

A
Back

ꓱ
Front

ꓱ
Back

D
Back

Ouranosaurus

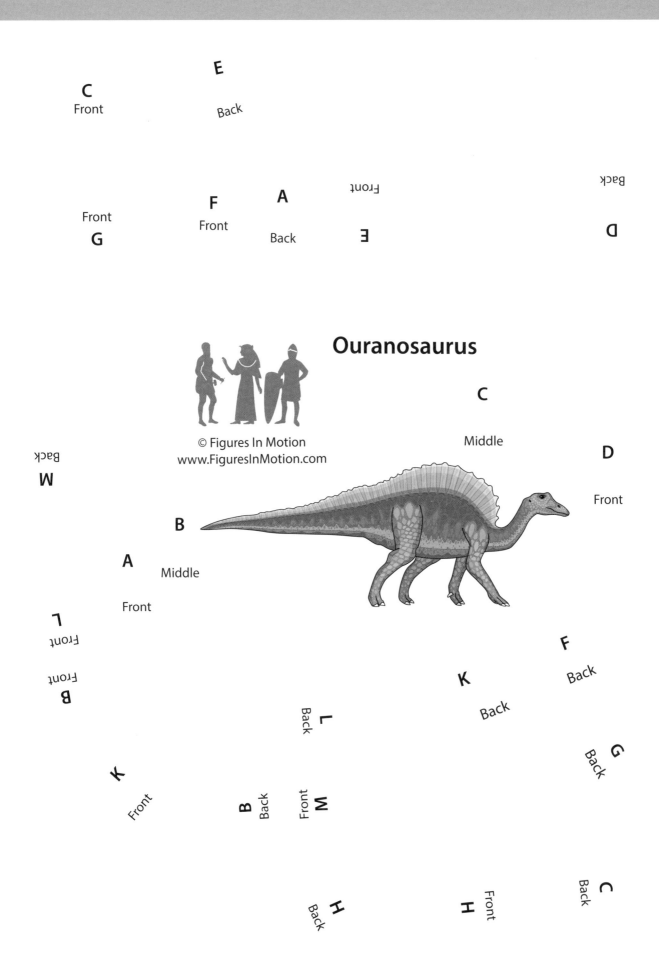

© Figures In Motion
www.FiguresInMotion.com

W
Back

C
Middle

D
Front

B

A
Middle

Front

ꓶ
Front

B
Front

K
Back

F
Back

K
Front

L
Back

B
Back

W
Front

G
Back

H
Back

H
Front

C
Back

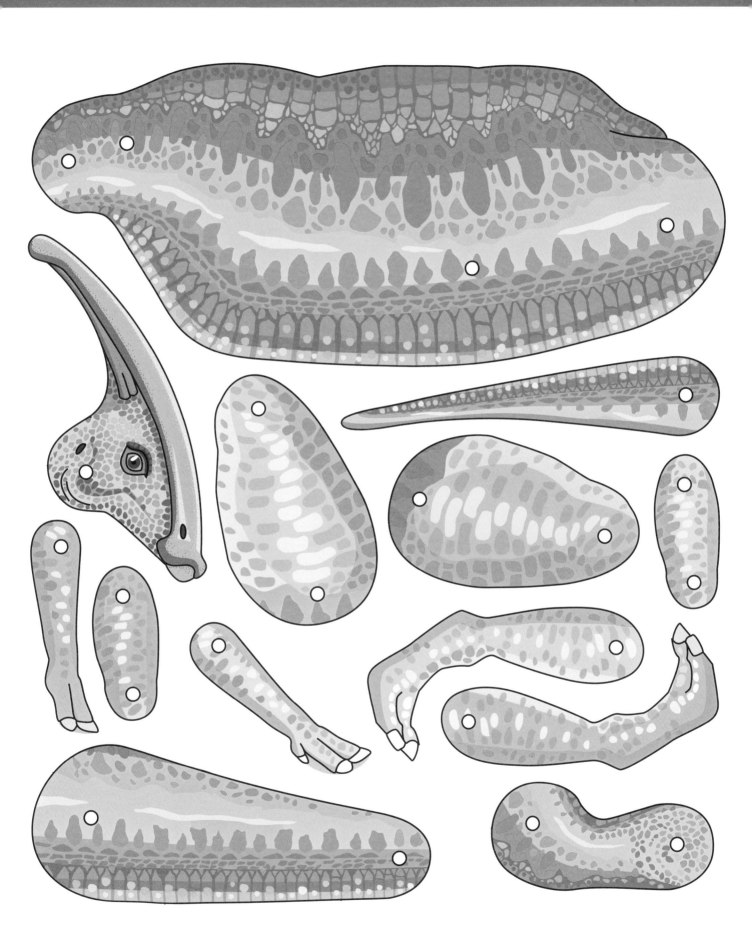

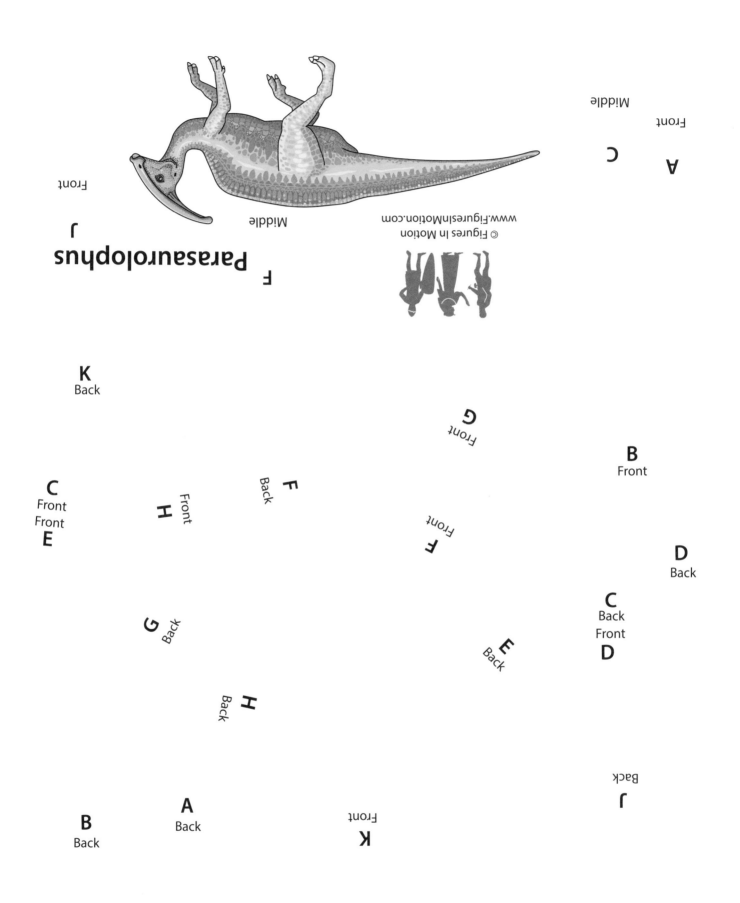

Parasaurolophus

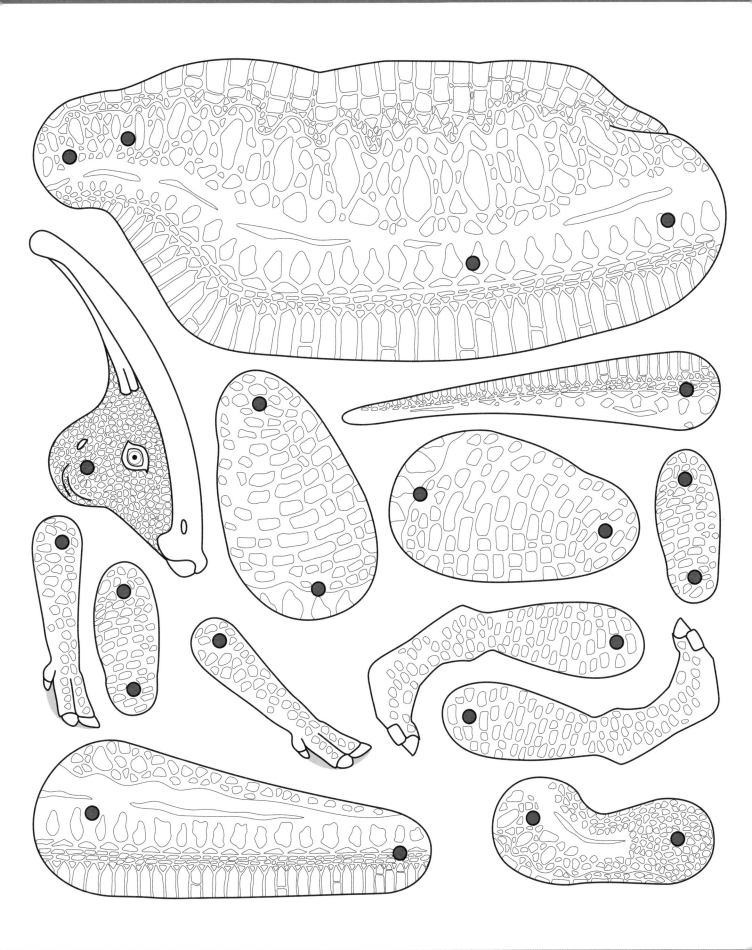

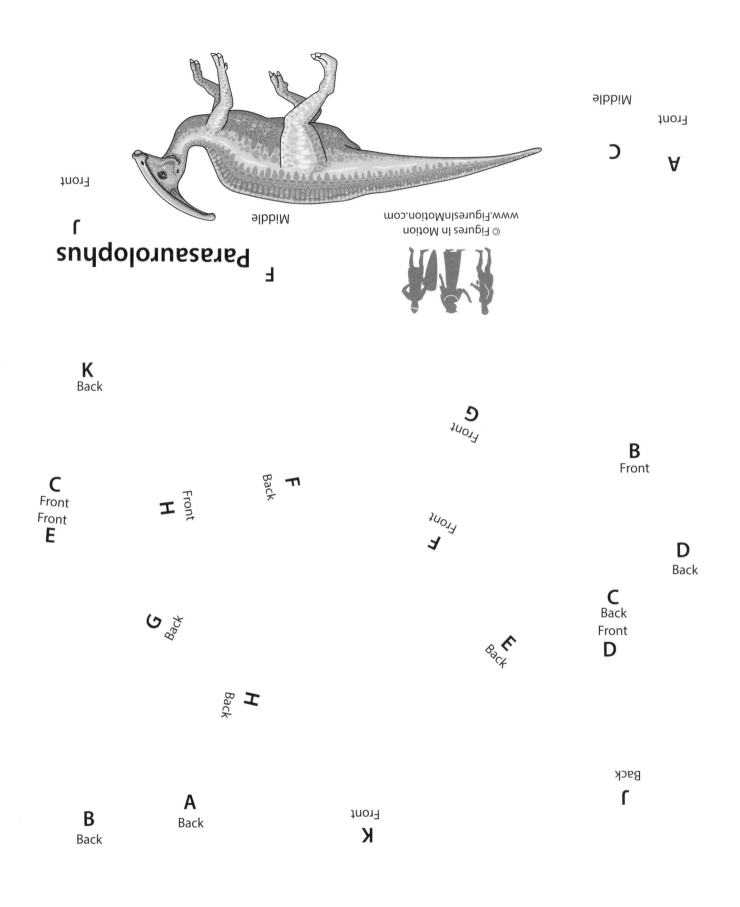

J **Parasaurolophus** F

Front

Middle

Front

Middle

A C

Front

© Figures In Motion
www.FiguresInMotion.com

K
Back

G
Front

B
Front

C
Front
Front
E

F
Back

H
Front

F
Front

D
Back

C
Back
Front
D

G
Back

E
Back

H
Back

J
Back

B
Back

A
Back

K
Front

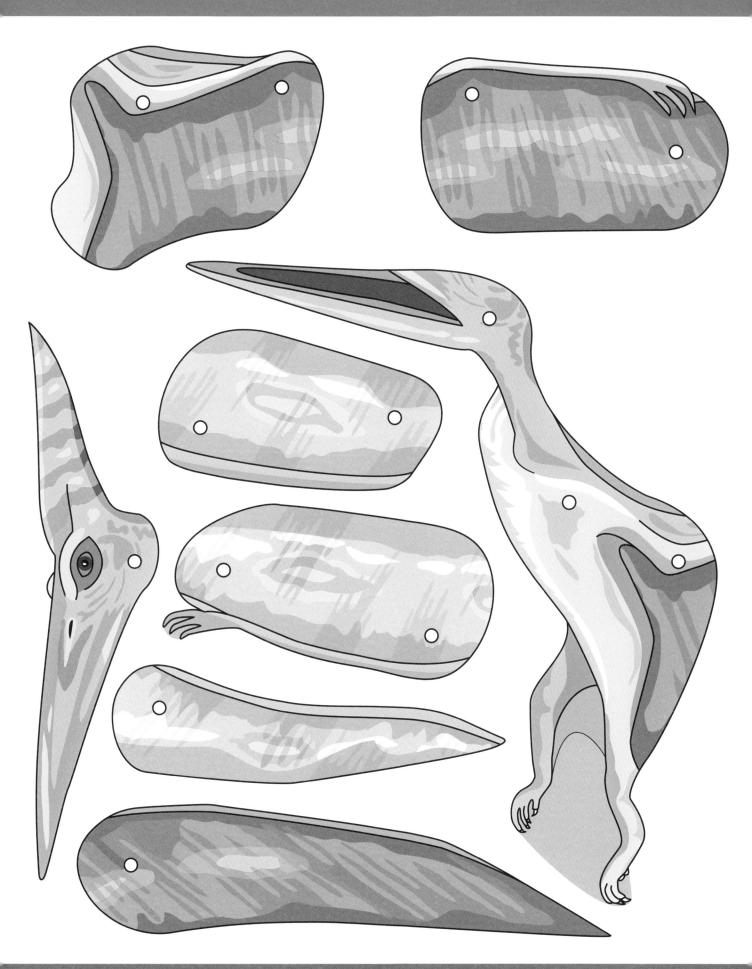

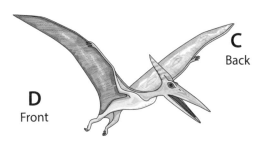

C
Back

D
Front

C
Front

B
Back

© Figures In Motion
www.FiguresInMotion.com

A

Back

F

Front

E
Back

E
Front

Pteranodon

B
Front

G

Front

A
Front

F

Back

Back

G

D

Back

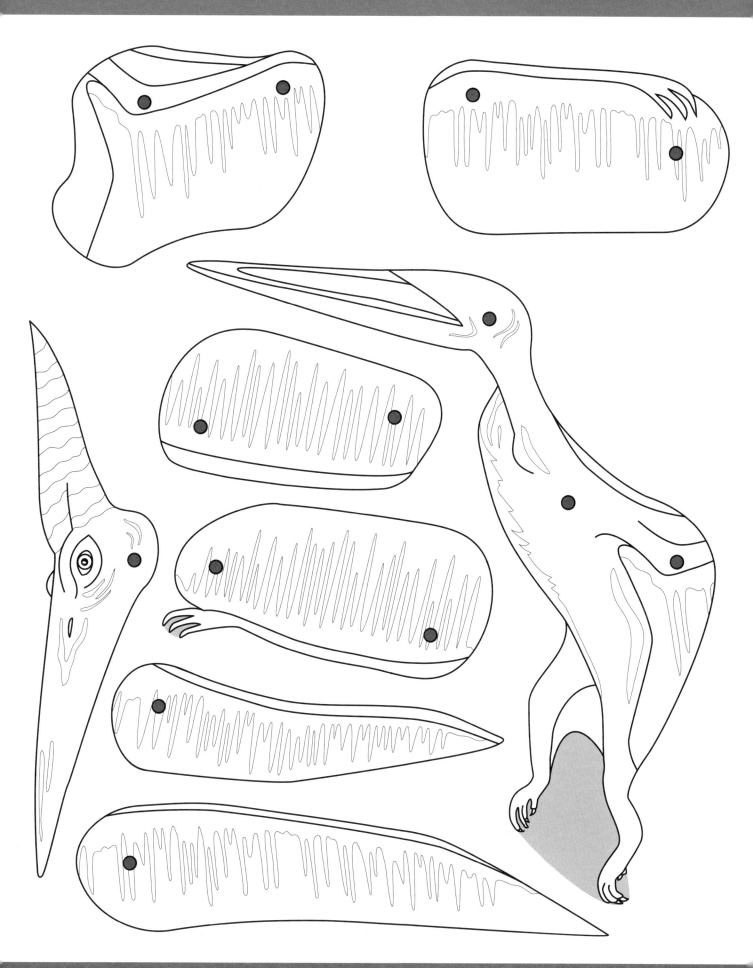

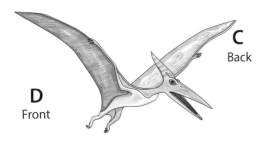

C
Back

D
Front

C
Front

B
Back

© Figures In Motion
www.FiguresInMotion.com

A

Back

F

Front

E
Back

E
Front

Pteranodon

G

A
Front

F

B
Front

Front

Back

Back

G

D

Back

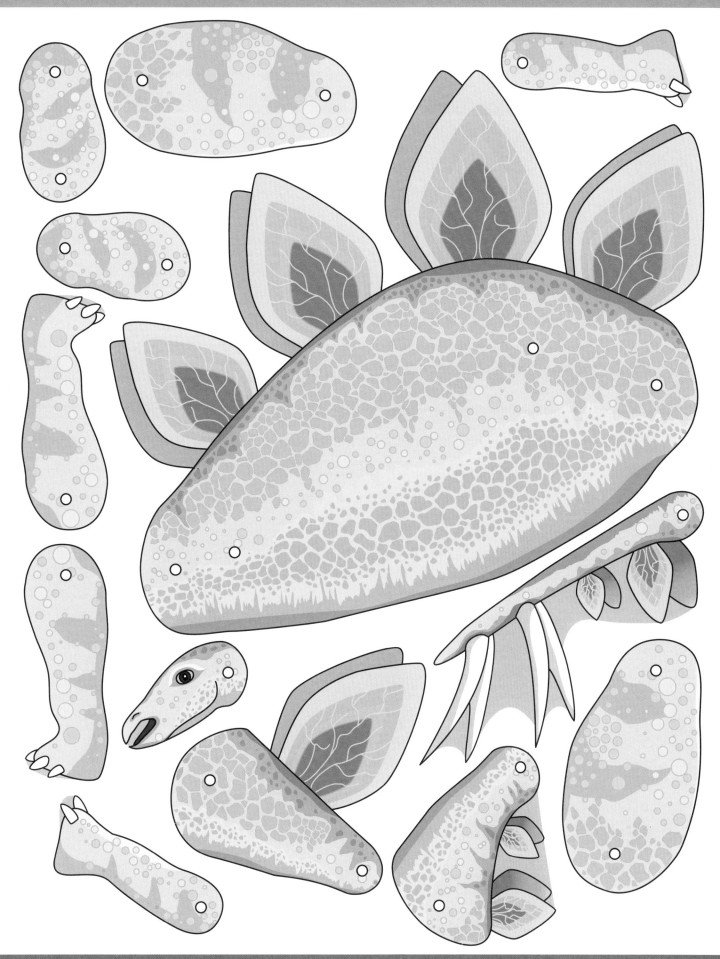

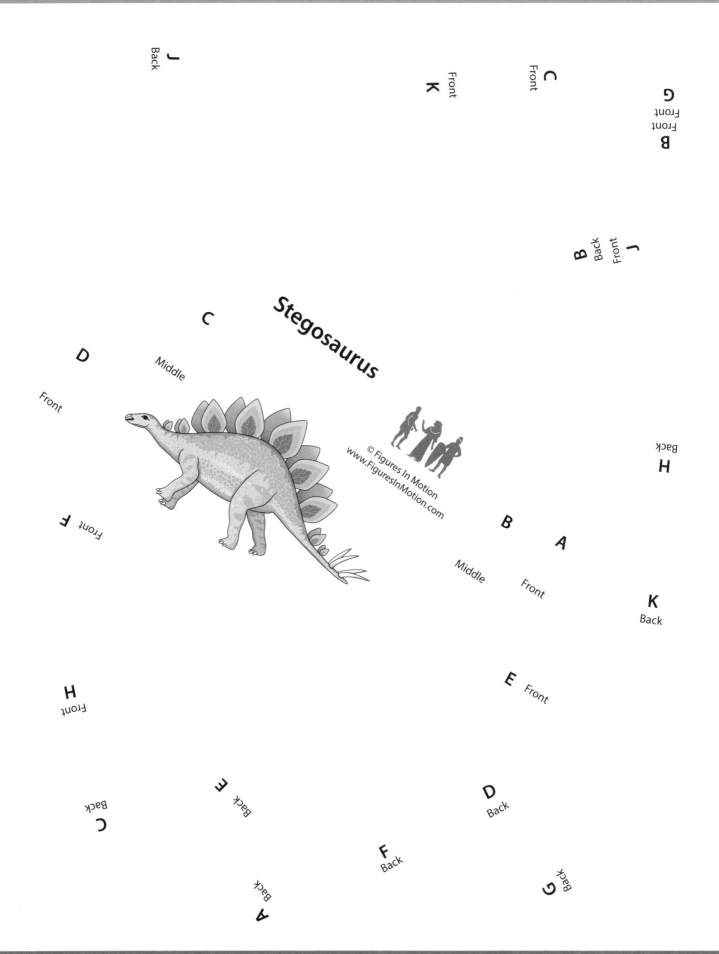

Stegosaurus

© Figures In Motion
www.FiguresInMotion.com

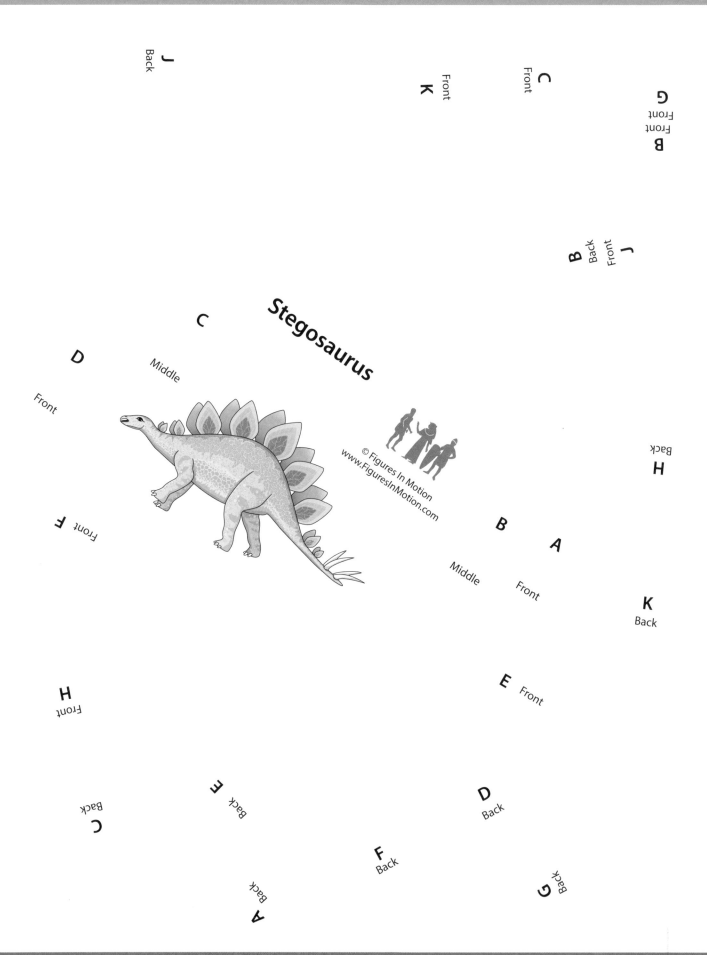

Stegosaurus

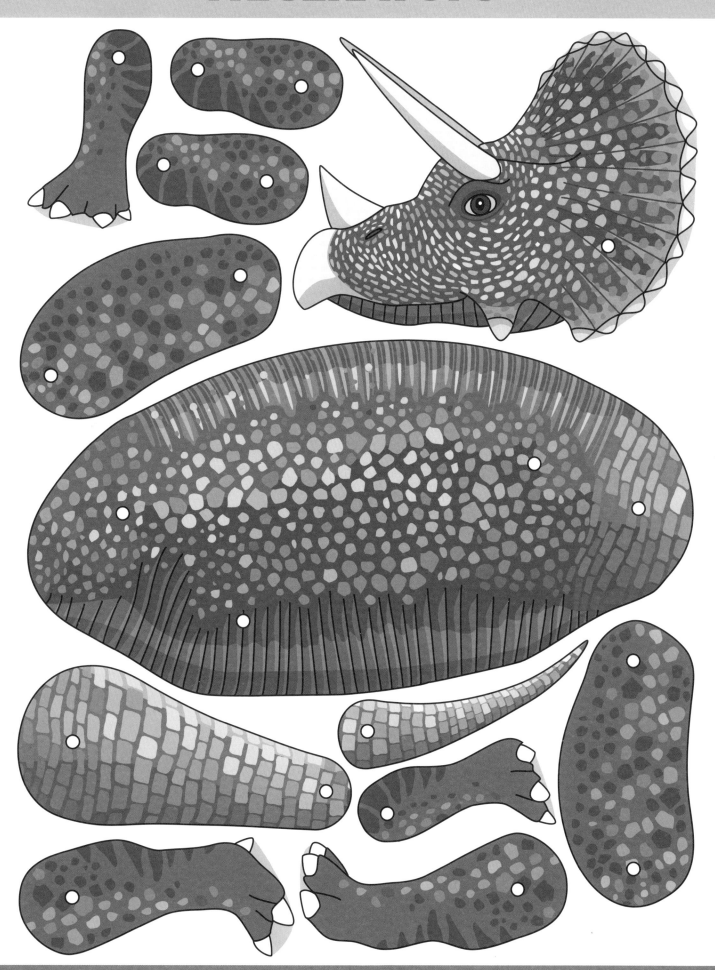

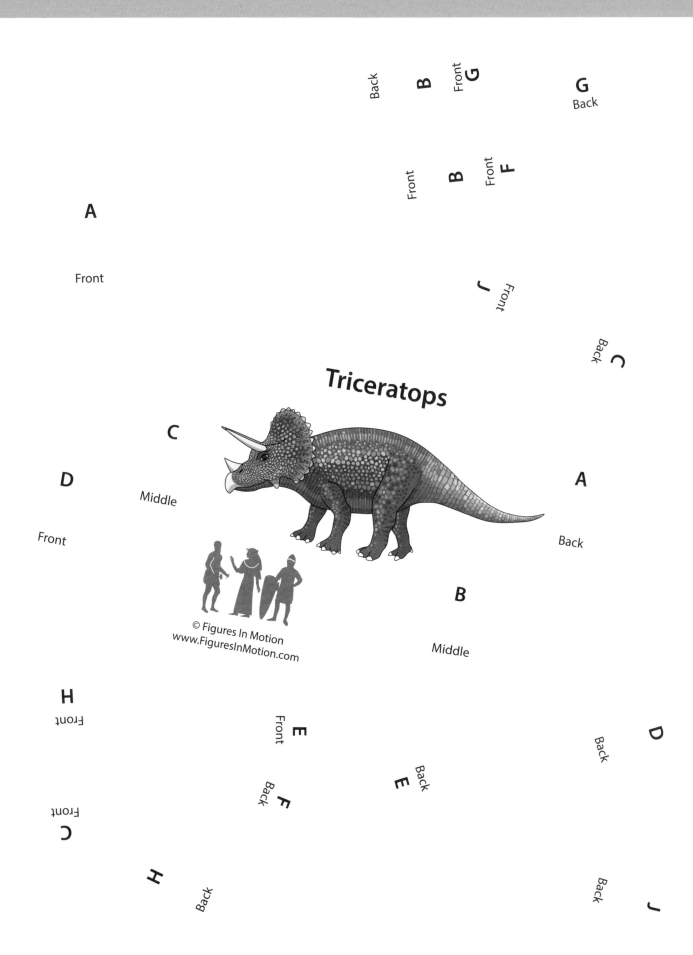

Triceratops

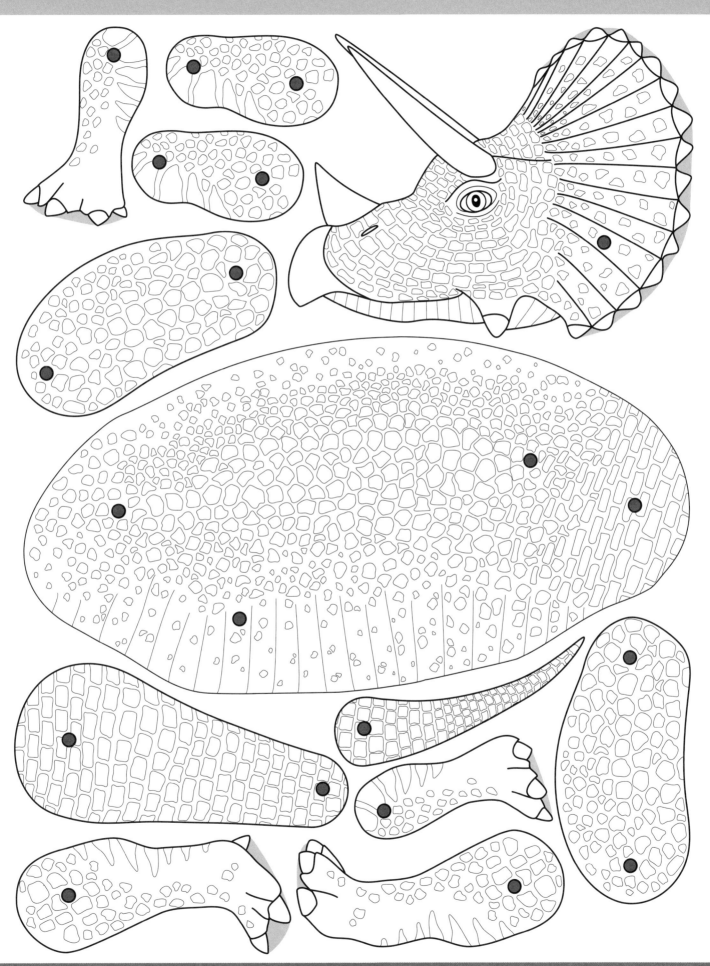

Triceratops

Back

B

Front **G**

G
Back

Front

B

Front **F**

A

Front

J

Front

Back

C

C

Middle

D

Front

A

Back

© Figures In Motion
www.FiguresInMotion.com

B

Middle

H

Front

Front

E

Front

D

Back

C

Back **F**

E

Back

H

Back

J

Back

TYRANNOSAURUS REX

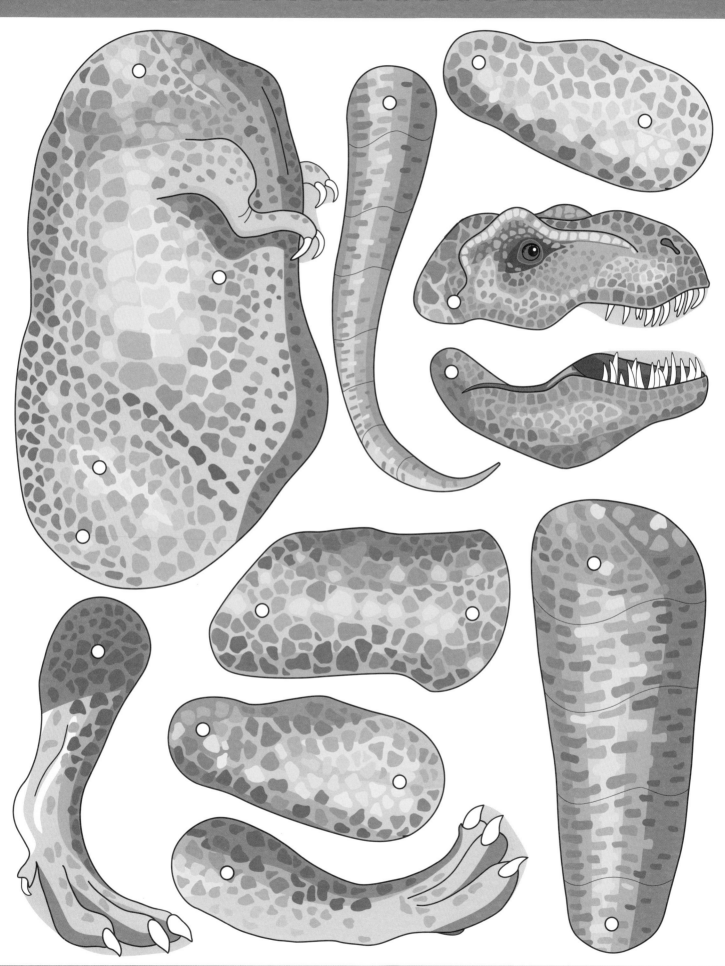

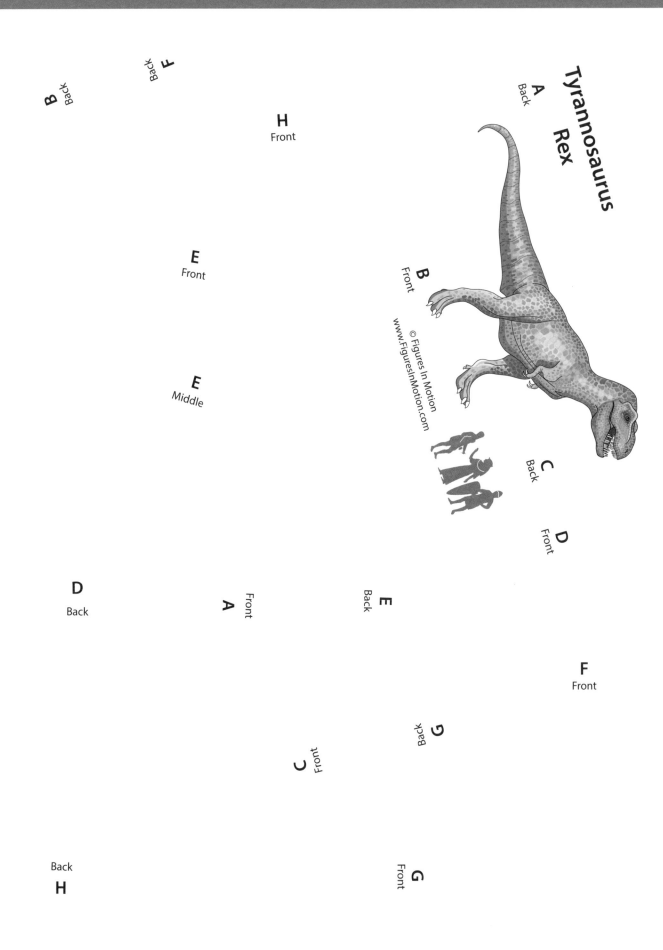

B
Back

F
Back

H
Front

Tyrannosaurus Rex
A
Back

E
Front

B
Front

© Figures In Motion
www.FiguresInMotion.com

E
Middle

C
Back

D
Front

D
Back

A
Front

E
Back

F
Front

G
Back

C
Front

G
Front

H
Back

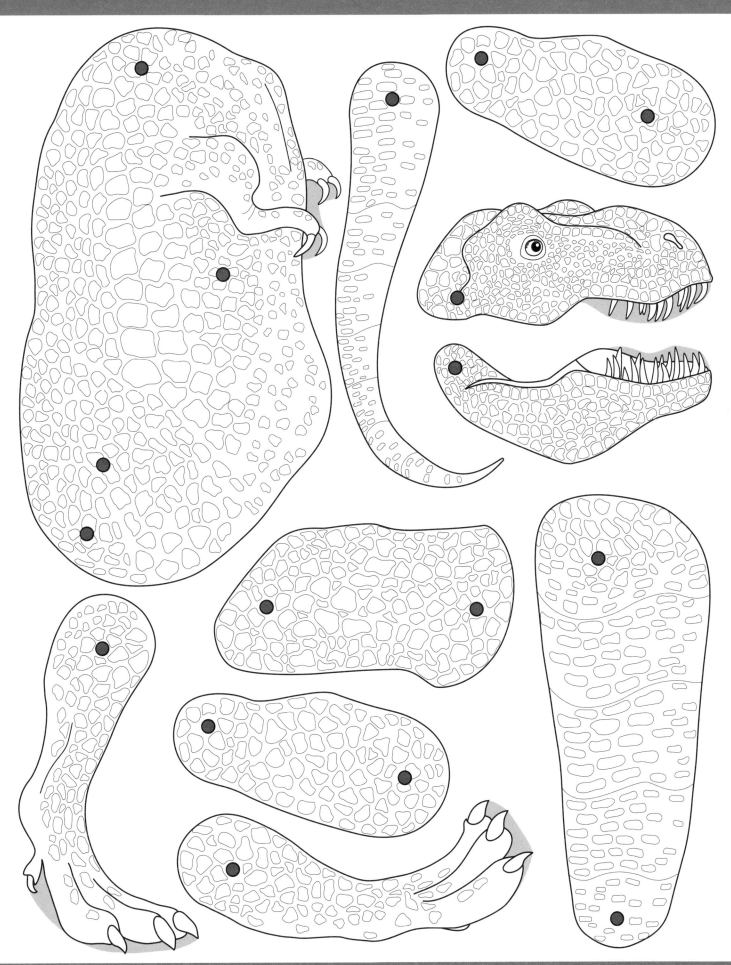

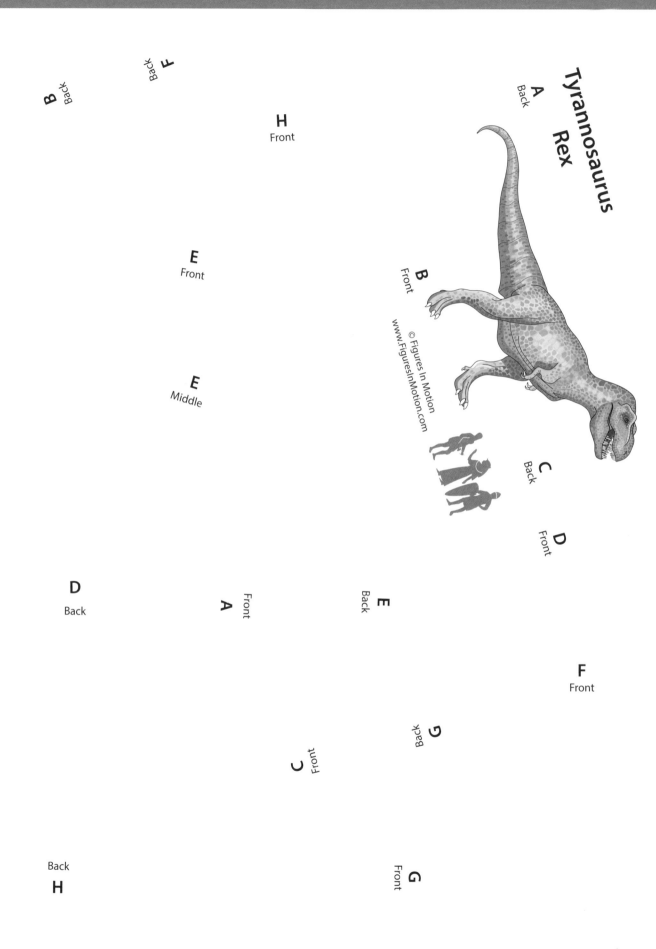

Tyrannosaurus
Rex

A
Back

B
Back

F
Back

H
Front

E
Front

E
Middle

B
Front

© Figures In Motion
www.FiguresInMotion.com

C
Back

D
Front

D
Back

A
Front

E
Back

F
Front

C
Front

G
Back

G
Front

H
Back

Make an Articulated Dinosaur

Making an articulated dinosaur puppet is easy. Before getting started, gather the following: coloring supplies (crayons, colored pencils, markers, or paint), scissors, ⅛" hole punch with a 1" reach, and mini brads (⅛") or brass fasteners. Note: When using brass fasteners to assemble the figures, a standard hole punch may be used.

COLOR

- Use crayons, colored pencils, markers, or paint to color the figures.

CUT

- Remove the page of the figure to be assembled by tearing at the perforation along the book spine.
- Cut out each of the figure pieces. To make cutting easier, younger children can cut outside the shaded areas around intricate parts.
- Punch out the holes for the mini brads with a hole punch. The holes are colored red in the black-and-white figures to make hole identification easier.

ASSEMBLE

- Place the figure pieces face down (back side up) so that the assembly letters and figure name are visible.
- Match the letters together. A Front goes with A Back. B Front goes with B Back, etc.
- Place the pieces marked Front under the pieces marked Back as you look at the back side of the figure. Place the pieces marked Middle between the Front and Back pieces.
- Double check to make sure that all of the letters are matched together and that they are in the correct order. Some figures have more than two pieces that will be attached by one mini brad.
- Insert the mini brad from the front side of the figure into the holes of the pieces to be joined together. The prongs of the mini brad should come out of the back side of the figure pieces.
- Separate the two prongs. Press them flat on the back side of the figure.
- Repeat until all of the holes are joined with mini brads.
- The figure is assembled. Have fun playing!

About the Author

In addition to creating dinosaur puppets, Cathy Diez-Luckie is dedicated to providing parents and teachers with history activities that excite creative children and reluctant learners. Her articulated paper puppets of famous people make learning fun while sharpening a child's story telling abilities and fine motor skills.

"The study of history can be more than a reading or listening activity. It can be engaging and memorable. It can be designed to spark the imagination while developing curious and competent learners," explains Diez-Luckie. Cathy's goal is to create meaningful and easy-to-use activities that will ignite a child's interest in history and encourage them to discover more about the great men and women of the past.

Cathy's movable historical figures have become a popular accompaniment to any history curriculum as they bring to life time periods such as ancient and medieval times, the Renaissance, the American Revolution, the Civil War period, and the early modern era. Cathy's next book will cover the famous people of modern times.

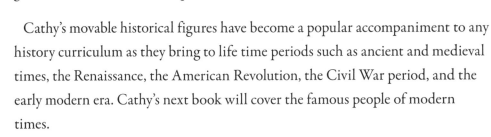

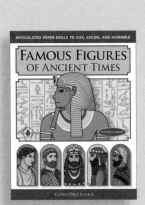
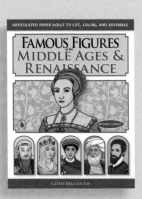
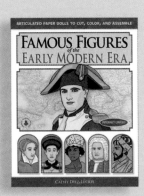
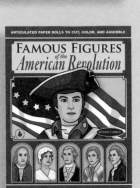
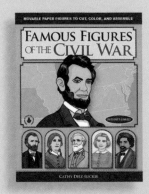
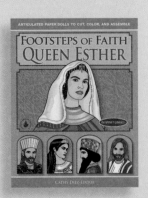